Grade 3.2

Scott Foresman

Decodable
Practice Readers
16 - 30
Volume 2

Scott Foresman
is an imprint of

Glenview, Illinois • Boston, Massachusetts • Chandler, Arizona
• Upper Saddle River, New Jersey

ISBN-13: 978-0-328-49219-0
ISBN-10:   0-328-49219-1

2 3 4 5 6 7 8 9 10 V011 14 13 12 11 10
CC1

Contents

UNIT 6

A Party for the Geese

Written by Kenneth Freid

Irregular Plurals

men	women	knives
children	leaves	geese
people	loaves	wolves

High-Frequency Words

the	a	to
water	of	people
two	said	one
what	where	laughed
was	they	have
their	watched	

1

Each summer the Glendale Street families held a big party. On a bright June day, everybody gladly marched to Blake Pond. Men carried large boxes filled with cold drinks. Women carried big baskets and bags filled with lunch, plates, cups, forks, and knives. Children carried gear for playing games.

The pond looked peaceful. Soft breezes ruffled leaves. Ducks floated on the pond. Big, loud geese waded in the water.

"Let's play a game," Jeff Sanders suggested. "We've got plenty of people for two teams."

"We can leave lunch on the tables," Mrs. Perez said.

"I'm not playing," Mrs. Wong said, "so I will set up the tables."

The neighbors played a lively game. One team scored six runs. The other team scored seven runs.

"I'm starved!" Kelly Wong finally yelled. "It's lunchtime!"

Men, women, and children quickly went back to the tables. Then everybody saw a strange sight.

4

Mrs. Wong stood near the tables looking unhappy. Crackers and loaves of bread lay nearby. Seven geese honked loudly.

Everybody spoke at the same time. "What happened? What's going on? Where's lunch?"

Mrs. Wong laughed. "It looks as if wild wolves chased me. But it was really just these geese," she said.

"But let me tell you what happened. I was just taking bags of crackers and loaves of bread to the tables. Seven geese came running, honking loudly. More followed them. I tripped over geese. I waved bags to make them leave, but then a bag broke. Crackers and bread tumbled out. I got upset, but those silly geese seemed really happy!"

Everybody laughed. Mrs. Wong felt fine. They still had plenty of lunch for everybody.

6

"I think Mrs. Wong has been really helpful," Mr. Perez said. "Now those geese can have their own meal. They will let us enjoy our party!"

The families ate salads, chicken, potatoes, pickles, peaches, and apples. Everybody enjoyed lunch.

After eating, the neighbors watched the geese. They seemed to enjoy parties too!

Camping!

Irregular Plurals

men	women	children
fish	shelves	feet
moose	oxen	geese
mice	wolves	

High-Frequency Words

was	a	the	women
they	of	to	come
here	are	many	do
said	one	from	we're
there	live		

Vic Solo was a firefighter and a dad. He came home with news for his boys. He had the next five days off. All men and women firefighters rotate shifts so they can spend long chunks of time with family.

"Jake! Dom!" Dad called to his children. "Come on down here. I've got news."

Jake and Dom came running.

"Boys, the time has come for the three Solo men to take a camping trip," stated Dad.

"We are the Solo men! And that sounds like fun!" shouted Dom. "Will we get to go fishing?"

"We will!" replied Dad. "How many fish do you think we'll reel in?"

"I think I'll bring in five fish," said Dom.

"I'll get nine fish," bragged Jake.

"Well, then I'll just need one fish," joked Dad. "And we'll eat like kings."

The men began to pack. Each got a bag from the shelves. Dad reached for his from the top shelf.

"Pack good socks!" Dad told his boys. "It's important that our feet stay dry while camping. Just one wet foot can make for a bad time."

"Dad, will we see a moose while camping?" asked Dom.

"We might," replied Dad. "If we're lucky we might get to see five or six moose!"

"How about an ox?" asked Jake.

"There are no oxen there," Dad said, grinning.

The Solo men did see a moose! Plus, they spotted a big goose and a bunch of baby geese. Jake even spotted a mouse under a leaf. Then Dom spotted three more mice in a pile of leaves! Dad joked that he saw a wolf. But the boys knew that wolves didn't live around here.

It was a fantastic camping trip!

Sheep Stampede

Irregular Plurals

children	calves	people
oxen	sheep	hooves

High-Frequency Words

the	to	a	what
said	any	today	who
of	why	people	something
many	two	are	they
one	from	there	were

This is the day for Miss Baxter's big class trip to a farm! Miss Baxter had her children read about farm animals before this trip. As her children rode that bus, Miss Baxter quizzed them.

"What is a baby cow called?" asked Miss Baxter. Tina raised her hand.

"A baby cow is a calf," said Tina. "Will we see any calves at this farm today?"

"I can't say," replied Miss Baxter. "We'll see. Now, who can tell me what kind of strong cow is used to pull carts?"

11

Miss Baxter's class went silent.

"This kind of cow has big horns," added Miss Baxter. "In class we saw that film about them. This cow helped pull tree trunks in a forest."

Cathy raised her hand.

"Is it an ox?" she asked.

"Yes," Miss Baxter stated. "An ox. That's why people might say that something is 'strong as an ox.' Many times, two oxen are needed for pulling big carts."

Just then, the bus stopped. The children got off the bus at Farmer Bill's. As they waited for Farmer Bill, Tina walked to a fence. Tina spotted one sheep standing by that fence.

Tina saw that this sheep had a rock stuck in its hoof. Tina opened the gate to help that sheep. Suddenly, the sound of lots and lots of hooves made the ground shake! Twenty sheep came running out of that barn. They were all going to escape from the gate!

Farmer Bill came over just in time! He shut that gate. No sheep escaped! Tina told Farmer Bill that she spotted a rock in the hoof of one sheep. Farmer Bill fixed that sheep right up!

There were no close calls for the rest of the trip. The class had a good time on the farm.

Whirling Girl

Written by Jennifer Hills

R-controlled *ir, er, ur, ear, or, ar, ore, oar*

Shirley	start	her	far	early	morning
short	born	whirl	Earth	word	smart
girl	learned	Park	soaring	hurl	sport
chores	certain	more	serve	world	first
burst	bird	dirt	wore	store	yard
porch	works	roared	garden	blurted	story
turn	sorted	twirl	harm	perfect	order
large	Mort	worn	before	sir	perform
pearls	sparkled	circled			

High-Frequency Words

from	the	one
was	to	what
who	of	put
could	do	into
were	wanting	you
said	they	have

Shirley had talent. From the start, her Mom and Dad felt that she might go far. Early one morning a short time after she was born, Shirley began to whirl. Mom and Dad saw her spinning like a top in her crib.

"What on Earth!" exclaimed Dad.

"My word!" cried Mom.

Shirley was a smart girl who liked helping out.
But she felt happiest when spinning. She learned
to use her spinning in lots of ways. In City Park,
she gave kids soaring rides. She learned to hurl
the shot put far. That seemed like her best sport!
And at home, Shirley helped her dad with chores.

But Shirley felt certain she could do more. Might her talent for spinning help serve the world?

Shirley dreamed a dream. In her dream, she became Whirling Girl! At first, she burst into the earth to save a bird trapped in dirt. Then in her dream, she whirled rope around men who wore masks. These men were robbing the safe in a store.

Shirley woke up wanting to be Whirling Girl! In the yard near her porch, she tied spades to her feet. She started to spin.

"If this works, I bet I can dig to the far side of the world!"

"What are you doing?" roared Dad.

"You dug holes in my garden!" yelled Mom.

Shirley blurted out the story of her dream.

"Shirley," said Mom, "you don't have to whirl and turn to be great. We think you're great no matter what!"

Mom and Dad hugged Shirley. Then they sat down and sorted out ways to help Shirley twirl, turn, and whirl without harm.

Mom and Dad had the perfect plan! They placed an order for ice skates!

Later at a large ice rink, Shirley met a skating coach named Mort. They started skating.

"Have you ever worn skates before?" asked Coach Mort.

Shirley said, "No, sir."

"I have never seen a girl learn to skate so fast!" he exclaimed.

In no time, Shirley was set to perform. She wore a skating dress with pearls and sequins. She sparkled like a star as she circled the ice. But the crowd enjoyed it most when Shirley, the Whirling Girl, twirled like a top!

20

Mom's Purse

Vowels: r-Controlled /er/ spelled _ir, er, ur,_

ear, or and _ar, or, ore, oar_

year	Stark	stores	outskirts	sporting	oar	for
burst	splinters	during	storm	yarn	her	scarves
skirts	sorts	starts	third	markers	gear	art
horn	uniform	tore	arm	near	parks	car
purse	turn	cards	uproar	ears	hard	Dear
counter	rear	wore	dark	star	patterns	birthday
shirt	perturbed	work				

High-Frequency Words

the	a	to	of	into	have
they	other	from	you	sure	your
says	said				

Each year, the Stark family takes a trip to the big outlet stores located on the outskirts of town.

This trip, Dad needs to visit the sporting goods store. He needs a new oar for his rowboat. His last oar burst into splinters during a storm.

Mom must stop at the yarn store. Mom runs a shop of her own. She sells things that she knits. She knits scarves and skirts. She knits all sorts of stuff!

21

The kids have stuff they must shop for as well. Bobby needs to get things for class. He starts third grade this year. He needs markers, paints, and other gear for art class.

Jill plays horn in her class band. But she needs a new jacket for her band uniform. She tore the arm on her old uniform.

The Starks are near the outlet stores. As Dad parks the car, Mom checks for her purse.

"Turn back," states Mom. "I forgot all my cash and credit cards!"

The uproar from the kids makes Dad put his hands on his ears.

"Are you sure?" asks Dad. "Look hard!"

"Yes, Dear," replies Mom. "I think my wallet is on that counter in the rear of our house."

"Did you leave it in that purse you wore last night?" asks Jill. "That purse with dark star patterns on it that you got for your birthday?"

"Yes," replies Mom. "That purse."

"Is it that purse that matches this shirt I have on?" asks Jill.

"Yes," says Mom. She's getting just a bit perturbed with Jill.

"Is it this purse that I'm holding?" asks Jill.

Mom turns to see that Jill has her purse. And inside is Mom's wallet!

"Nice work, Jill!" said Mom. "Now let's shop!"

Thursday's Roaring Storm

Vowels: r-Controlled /er/ spelled *ir, er, ur, ear, or* and *ar, or, ore, oar*

Thursday	storm	roared	Kirsten	tore	her
yard	turned	cars	fear	hurt	person
rear	hurled	burst	worst	start	shirt
chore	part	dirt	sorted	torn	corkboard
party	purse	parts	dark	for	hardware
store	morning	worn	near	farm	corn
stars	bird	soar	perched	skirt	scarf
after	snoring				

High-Frequency Words

a	into	of	was	one	the
to	do	been	two		

    Last Thursday, a big storm roared into Kirsten's town. It tore trees right out of her yard and turned cars upside down! Kirsten's big fear was that people in her town were hurt. Her town was lucky! Not one person was hurt.

    Kirsten's room sits in the rear of her house, next to the yard. That wind had hurled a tree limb at Kirsten's house. The limb had burst right into her bedroom window! It was the worst!

"Time to start cleaning," Mom told Kirsten. "Get on an old shirt and pants."

"Cleaning this will be quite a chore," Kirsten sighed. "But I'll do my part.

As Mom swept up dirt, Kirsten sorted her stuff. Photos had been torn off her corkboard, and her party purse was in two parts!

It got dark before Kirsten and Mom finished. Her room was clean, but her window was still broken.

"We'll close this door for the night," Mom told Kirsten. "Dad will visit the hardware store in the morning and get new glass."

"I'm worn out," stated Kirsten.

"Let's rest in the yard," smiled Mom.

Kirsten's house was near a farm. The storm had blown husks of corn into her yard. It was a mess!

As Kirsten and Mom sat in the yard, they gazed up at the stars. Just then Kirsten spotted a bird soar at her house.

"Mom! That bird is perched in my window!" yelled Kirsten. "What if it makes a nest with my best skirt or my scarf?"

"That bird needs to rest after the storm, too," said Mom. "I think I hear it snoring!"

Kirsten giggled with Mom. Kirsten let the tired bird rest.

Midsummer Fun

Written by Neil Fairbairn

Prefixes *pre-, mid-, over-, out-, bi-, de-*

outdoors	bicycle	outline
outside	midpoint	presoak
overcrowded	midsummer	overgrown
overhead	defrost	

High-Frequency Words

do	you	have
a	to	of
what	are	the
pull	into	two
water	your	ones
they	want	

25

Do you have a green thumb? Then try gardening for a fun way to spend time outdoors. You can get lots of fresh air—and things to eat. Think about what you can grow: peas, peppers, carrots, berries, and more.

I think beans are best. You can eat them and play with them as well. That's right, play with them. Here's how.

First, ride your bicycle to a garden shop and pick up a packet of pole bean seeds. Also get six thin poles, each at least six feet long.

Next, set up the planting space in the garden. On the ground, outline a circle three feet wide. Then pull weeds and turn over the dirt inside the circle with a garden fork.

Rake the ground flat. Then place six poles around the outside of the circle with their tops leaning into the midpoint. Leave a bigger space between two poles. Why? Wait and see!

Tie the pole tops with string. Now you've got a pole frame.

When days start getting hot in late spring, presoak your bean seeds. Plant them by placing six beans at the base of each pole and poking them an inch into the ground. Place dirt over them and water them daily.

In less than ten days, your bean plants will sprout.

When the bean plants are three inches high, thin them out. Take out the little ones, and leave three strong plants at each pole. The plants must not be overcrowded.

Keep sprinkling them with water, and see how fast they grow. Your plants will race up the poles.

By midsummer your bean plants will reach
pole tops. The frame will be overgrown with big
leaves and bright flowers. These flowers will turn
into beans you can eat.

Now can you see why you left space between
two poles? It's an opening for your pole bean
tent!

Your bean tent is like a house with leaves and flowers growing overhead. It is a place for shade on a hot day. It is a place to play hide-and-seek or just sit inside and read.

It has plenty of green beans to pick and eat. And if you want to eat your beans during the winter, save them in the freezer. Be sure to defrost them before eating!

A Midsummer Visit

Prefixes *pre-*, *mid-*, *over-*, *out-*, *bi-*, *de-*

biweekly	overlooks	midsummer
preflight	overbooked	overcrowded
outside	midday	midwinter
deicing	deactivate	oversize
Midwest	precooked	overeat
outstanding		

High-Frequency Words

to	a	the	of
you	your	are	they
said	was		

This will be Beth's first plane trip ever! She and Mom will fly to see Gramps. He has a home in the state of Maine. In his biweekly phone call with Beth, Gramps invited her for a visit.

"My home overlooks a lake," explained Gramps. "It's so nice in midsummer. You and your mom need to visit!"

Now Beth and Mom are about to go! They are eating a preflight snack. The plane will be set to board soon. Mom hopes the plane isn't overbooked.

"Overbooked means that too many tickets were sold," explains Mom. "Overcrowded flights are less fun."

A voice sounds on the loudspeaker. "Now boarding, flight nine. Flight nine, now boarding."

"That's us," smiles Mom.

Beth and Mom get in line. In no time, they are on the plane and in their seats. Beth has a window seat. She looks outside at the midday sun. It's a clear day for flying! She is glad. Mom said that if it was midwinter, ice might have to be cleaned off the wings. That's called deicing.

A voice spoke on the plane's loudspeaker. "We will be taking off shortly. Please deactivate all cell phones. Please bring oversize bags to the back of this plane. Seat backs and tray tables need to be upright. Thanks for flying with us!"

Beth is ready. Before she knows it, her plane is in the sky! Beth looks out her window. "It's neat to see the Midwest from way up high," Beth tells Mom.

A precooked meal is set on Beth's tray. Beth eats a bit. She does not wish to overeat.

The plane lands in Maine. Gramps greets Beth and Mom. "How was your flight?" he asks.

"Outstanding!" replies Beth.

Spelling Bee

Prefixes *pre-, mid-, over-, out-, bi-, de-*

outstanding	dethroned	pretest
midwinter	midday	overcast
overcoat	precooked	overcook
preheat	defrost	midway
biped	decode	overconfident
misspell	midmorning	Biplane
overhead	midword	overcome

High-Frequency Words

was	the	of	want
to	a	said	anything
two	wasn't	again	

Next Friday was the big third-grade spelling bee. Frank was an outstanding speller. Last year, he was the second-grade champ, the king of spellers! But he didn't want to be dethroned as king in the third grade. So he filled his pretest days with study!

But studying spelling words made Frank act strangely. He spelled words all the time! When he looked outside the window, he spelled *midwinter, midday, overcast,* and *overcoat.*

Then all week at mealtimes Frank spelled cooking words such as *precooked, overcook, preheat,* and *defrost.*

Frank had fun with spelling too. Midway on the walk to school, he called his sister a *biped* and spelled it for her. That made her mad! She thought *biped* meant an animal. Frank said, "Allow me to decode that word for you. *Biped* means 'Anything that walks on two feet.'"

On Friday, Frank sounded a bit overconfident about the spelling bee. Mom told him that might make him spell too quickly and misspell a word.

At midmorning, the spelling bee started. When it was Frank's first turn, his teacher said, "*Biplane.* A biplane flew overhead."

Frank smiled. This was easy. He quickly started to spell, "b-y-".

Frank stopped midword. That wasn't right! He started again, "b-i-p-l-a-n-e."

That was right! And so was Mom. Frank had to overcome being overconfident if he wanted to stay the champ.

Teller, Tailor, Seller, Sailor

Written by K. E. Theroux

Suffixes *-er, -or, -ess, -ist*

teacher	artist	actress	editors
conductors	driver	writer	inventor
firefighter	chemist		

High-Frequency Words

are	people	do
a	what	said
you	the	of
two	wants	watched
their	should	they
to	would	your

"Now we'll discuss jobs," Miss Lim told her class on Friday morning after math. "We know that jobs are things that people do for a living, so first tell me what my job is."

Lola spoke quickly, "You're a teacher, Miss Lim."

"And what do teachers do?" asked Miss Lim.

"Teachers help us learn things," Jeb finally blurted out.

"Now think about more jobs that people do when they grow up," Miss Lim said, handing out paper.

"After picking one job, you'll write about that job and tell why you picked it." Little by little the room grew silent as the class started making lists of jobs.

Rose can see herself in two jobs. First, she is an artist, and she paints big red flowers and yellow suns on large white canvases. People admire her bright paintings.

Then she is an actress, and she speaks her lines in plays on stage without making a single mistake! People clap and whistle loudly for her.

Lola knows she wants a job in which she helps people.

Her uncle is a doctor, and her mom is a dentist. Lola has watched them both at work. Doctors help sick or hurt people, while dentists help people care for their teeth. Both are fine jobs, and both jobs help people. Which job should she pick?

Zan likes reading stories. Editors fix mistakes in stories before they get printed, so an editor will read lots of stories.

Zan likes listening to music. Conductors lead bands when they play, so a conductor will listen to lots of music. Which job would be better for him?

First, Jeb sees himself as a racecar driver. He sees a sleek car speeding on a racetrack, and he holds the wheel tightly as he wins the race!

Then Jeb sees himself as a teacher. He sees happy kids sitting in a classroom, and he helps them learn things—just like Miss Lim!

"Now, class," said Miss Lim. "Let's start writing. Has everybody picked a job?"

"Actress! Writer! Dentist! Inventor! Firefighter! Sailor! Conductor! Seller! Chemist! TEACHER!"

Miss Lim smiled and held up her hands. "My, you're eager to write about your jobs! Now let's see that in your writing."

Spring Show

Suffixes -er, -or, -ess, -ist

teacher	director	actress	singer
announcer	speaker	hostess	artists
painters	graders	editor	reporter
dancers	seamstress	leader	soloist
vocalist	actors		

High-Frequency Words

the	a	to	you	they
of	have	one	whole	give

Each spring, the third-grade class has a fun show filled with songs and skits. Miss Phillips, the third-grade teacher, is this show's director.

Ellie is in Miss Phillips's class. When Ellie grows up, she hopes to be a singer, an actress, or an announcer. Miss Phillips asks Ellie to be the show's announcer.

"That means that you will be the main speaker," explains Miss Phillips. "You will announce each act and be the show's hostess."

Ellie works hard with Miss Phillips to make this show perfect. Ellie finds artists and painters to make the set. They are third graders too.

Miss Phillips and Ellie visit the editor of the town newspaper, *The Daily Times*. Ellie asks him to print an ad that invites the town to the show. The editor tells them he will send a reporter to see the show as well.

This show will have dancers. The day before the show, Miss Phillips sees that one of the dancers ripped his red shirt. Miss Phillips's sister is a seamstress. She quickly mends the little rip.

On the evening of the show, Ellie peeks out at the crowd. It looks like the whole town came out! Ellie even sees the town's leader!

Then it is time to start the show!

"Thanks for stopping by to see our show," Ellie tells the crowd. "Let's get started with a singing soloist. Please give a hand for our star vocalist, Kevin!"

After Kevin's song, Ellie introduces a skit. The actors tell jokes. The crowd giggles! People clap for act after act.

The third graders' spring show is a success!

A Princess or Not?

Suffixes -er, -or, -ess, -ist

reader	writer	cartoonist
princess	actress	visitor
inventor	stylist	

High-Frequency Words

a	to	the
of	far-off	sure
could	one	you
was	been	does
live	other	

Sam is a good reader. He likes to write too. Sam likes to write funny stories. He draws cartoons that match his stories. Sam plans to be a writer and cartoonist when he grows up.

Right now, Sam is reading a fairy tale. It's called "The Princess and the Pea." It tells the story of Princess Bo. Bo is stranded near Queen Jen's home. She asks Jen for a place to sleep that night. Bo explains that she is a princess from a far-off land.

Is Bo a real princess? Queen Jen isn't sure. Bo could be an actress playing one! The queen has a plan. She will let Bo sleep in a bed that is stacked with twenty mattresses! But under the bottom mattress, Jen hides a tiny pea. A true princess will be able to feel that tiny little pea.

"How did you sleep?" Queen Jen asks her visitor that next morning.

"At first, not well," explains Bo. "Until I reached under the bottom mattress and found this tiny pea. Then I slept quite well!"

Sam grinned as he read that and then turned to the last page in his book. The page was missing! It had been ripped out!

"But how does this story end?" asks Sam. "Wait! I'm a writer. I'll write my own ending!"

In Sam's ending, Queen Jen introduces Bo to her boy, Prince Boo. The prince and princess don't get married and live happily ever after like in other tales. Instead, Bo becomes a mattress inventor. She makes the best mattresses ever! And Boo becomes a blanket stylist. He designs blankets and sheets for Bo's mattresses.

Sam giggled at his ending. He can't wait to grow up and write silly stories and cartoons!

Miss Mildred's Ostrich

Written by Julie Renault

Syllable Pattern VCCCV

Constance	ostrich	Sandra	actress	constant
complain	Mildred	distress	frustrated	monster
control	inspect	complete	surprise	hungry
instant	hundred	impressed	exclaimed	

High-Frequency Words

friends	a	very
they	to	you
were	one	would
was	into	do
want		

Constance has a big dream. Her friends think it is a very strange dream. In fact, they think her plan is a little bird-brained. That's because Constance plans to own an ostrich farm!

"An ostrich farm?" Sandra asked. "Last time we talked you were going to be an actress!"

"That's a long story," Constance replied. She then told Sandra her long ostrich tale.

One day I heard an odd noise outside. That constant, loud noise went on and on, and soon I couldn't stand it a moment longer. I went to my window to complain. Little did I know as I opened the window that my goal in life would change.

Miss Mildred, the lady next door, had a huge crate in her yard. That knocking, banging noise came from inside her crate!

"Miss Mildred," I yelled over the racket. "Why is so much noise coming from that crate?"

The banging inside Miss Mildred's crate got louder.

Miss Mildred was in a state of distress! She was so frustrated that she burst into tears.

"Constance, my dear," she replied. "I don't know how to handle this mess! This monster is a birthday gift sent by my crazy Uncle Clem, but I cannot do a single thing to control it!"

Miss Mildred slumped down sadly on her knees.

I went out to inspect Miss Mildred's "monster."
When I peeked in the noisy crate, I got a
complete surprise.

"It's an ostrich!" I shouted, jumping back in
shock.

"Yes," Miss Mildred moaned, shaking her
head. "Please, can you help me with it?"

"Maybe it's hungry. When did it last eat?" I asked Miss Mildred, edging slowly closer.

Uncle Clem had sent big food bags with this crate. We gave that ostrich a nice snack. In an instant he was quiet. He made happy little sounds as he gobbled his food.

"It was such fun to help with that big bird," Constance said. "So now I am planning a huge ranch myself, with at least a hundred ostriches!"

Sandra was impressed by Constance's grand plan. "That's exciting!" Sandra exclaimed. "It sounds like fun."

"So, Sandra," Constance added with a wink, "do you want to help me work with the ostriches?"

Manfred's Monsters

Syllables VCCCV

Manfred's	Monsters	district	butterflies
complex	empty	hundreds	stretches
constant	improve	transformed	extra
instantly	complete	control	frustrated
benches	tangled	surprise	oddly
distract	exploded		

High-Frequency Words

hours	the	of	there
would	people	put	a
to	into	some	they
was	were	though	

Manfred's big indoor soccer game begins in just three hours. His team is called The Monsters. The winners of this game will be district champs! Nervous Manfred has butterflies in his tummy.

Manfred's mom and dad dropped him off at his sports complex. The stands in that complex were empty now. But later there would be hundreds of people in the seats!

As Manfred did his stretches, he remembered the years of constant hard work he put in. It took him a long time to improve. But he transformed himself into a fantastic player!

Before the game, Manfred and his team spent some extra time running drills. Then they went under the stands to relax a bit.

Soon it was time for this game to start. As the ref tossed out the ball, six players instantly made mad dashes for it. Manfred got there first. He made a few nice cuts in and out as he ran. He was in complete control of the ball. He took a shot, but just missed. That frustrated Manfred!

The game went on and on with no score. Players made nice passes, and when a team came close to getting a goal, players on both benches jumped up! But all shots were misses.

With just ten seconds left, the ball got loose. Manfred turned and ran right at it, but the laces on his sneakers got tangled. Manfred tripped and fell! To his surprise, the ball bounced oddly and landed right next to him. Manfred did not let tripping distract him, though. As he lay on the grass, Manfred swooped his leg around and kicked the ball at the goal. It went in!

The crowd exploded in happy yelling! The Monsters were district champs!

Winston's Complex Costume

Syllables VCCCV

Winston	pilgrim	pumpkin	monster
complex	instantly	startled	explore
purple	impress	children	frustrated
hundred	complains	complete	display
inspect	extra	hungry-looking	explode
exclaims	transforms	surprises	

High-Frequency Words

a	was	to	they	the
your	very	are	been	whole
two	comes	into		

Every October, Winston has a costume party. At last year's party, Winston dressed up as a pilgrim. The year before that, his costume was a pumpkin. This year, Winston plans to dress as a monster!

Winston asks his mom to help him get started on his costume.

"I'd like this outfit to be complex, Mom," Winston tells her. "I'd like my pals to be instantly startled when they see me!"

"Let's go explore the costume shops," suggests Mom.

In the first store, Winston asks the shopkeeper if he has a monster costume.

"Right this way," the shopkeeper replies. Then he points at a purple, fuzzy outfit. "This will impress your pals!"

Winston looks at the costume. It is nice, but not very frightening. Mom and Winston leave that store.

They go to store after store, but most of the costumes they see are for small children. Winston feels frustrated.

"I feel like we've been to a hundred shops," Winston complains.

But then it happens! Winston and Mom spot a shop with a complete monster outfit on display in the window.

"I'd like to inspect that outfit," Winston tells the man in this shop.

This outfit fits over Winston's whole body. It has two extra arms with big claws! The monster's teeth are hungry-looking fangs that seem to explode from the head!

"This costume is perfect!" exclaims Winston.

When the time for the party comes, Winston transforms himself into a terrifying monster. Winston surprises his pals with the best costume of the night!

60

Radio Days

Written by Corey Tenon

Syllable Pattern CV/VC

videos	stereo	recreation
radio	scientists	pianos
violins	pioneers	ideas
created	audio	audiences
dial		

High-Frequency Words

you	watch	to
the	people	of
have	would	your
their	they	were
could	one	new
some	laughed	

61

Did you watch videos last night? Maybe you listened to music on the stereo. Most people enjoy these forms of recreation. But sixty years ago or so, you might have spent time in different ways. You likely would have listened to your family's radio.

Back in those days, radio didn't just air music or news. Families gathered around big radios in their living rooms each night. They listened happily as actors and actresses performed plays, acted out stories, and cracked jokes. Sound effects made radio plays seem real.

How did radio start? Phones were invented in 1876. Phone signals went through wires. Scientists thought air, not wires, could carry radio signals. An inventor sent radio signals through air in 1895. Soon ships at sea could make calls with radios. Radio helped save shipwreck victims.

Before long, airplane pilots and armies used radios. Everybody called radio the *wireless* since radio waves moved through air without wires.

Music first aired on radio around 1910. It wasn't pop music but classical music, including pianos, violins, and singers. Before long, radio pioneers had new ideas and created all kinds of programs. Radio had audio for baseball games, news, and plays. Thrilling stories and funny comic shows became well-known.

One radio program called *The War of the Worlds* aired in 1938. It is still remembered. It described how beings from outer space invaded Earth. An emcee told this frightening story as if it were real. It scared thousands. It made some listeners panic.

Radio shows delighted audiences. In the daytime, children listened to shows made for kids. With the turn of a dial, families laughed at comic shows at night. Jack Benny and Bob Hope were well-known radio comics. Later, these comics became TV stars.

During the Second World War, radio gave audiences daily war news. Then big changes took place in the 1950s. Audiences began turning to TV. Music, news, and sports still aired on radio. But radio's golden age had ended.

Annual Music Fest

Syllable Pattern CV/VC

violin	annual	really	twentieth
champion	violinists	area	museum
create	twentieth	radio	dial
giant	created		

High-Frequency Words

a	the	today	of
one	to	was	whole
who	would	give	onto

Nell is feeling a bit uneasy. She plays the violin. Today she must play in the biggest show of her life. She must play at her town's annual music fest. And this year's show is really important. It is the twentieth annual music fest.

Every year at this fest, one grade school player is chosen to perform his or her music on stage. This year that player is Nell.

It was not easy to earn this spot. First at Nell's music school, she was named the champion violin player. And her school is filled with good violinists.

After that, Nell was named the champion violinist of the whole area! She beat many good players. That victory meant that she was the player who would perform in the annual fest.

The fest is held each year in back of the town's museum. It's a big deal for the whole town. The fest is even played over local radio.

Nell's music teacher had an idea. He asked Nell to create her own music for the fest. Nell liked to write music, so she agreed to create her own song.

At last, the town's twentieth annual music fest was underway. Nell was to go on soon. She was waiting backstage next to the radio. The radio dial was set on the show. Nell heard a voice on the radio say, "Next, please give a nice hand to Nell, our champion violinist!"

Nell grabbed her violin and ran onto the giant stage. She played the song she had created and then took a big bow. Nell had been tense, but she performed well. Nell now sat back and enjoyed the rest of her town's twentieth annual music fest.

Leona's Poem

Syllable Pattern CV/VC

poems	ideas	influence	poets
meteor	cruel	January	create
poem	punctuate	idea	Leona
museum	annual	lion	champion
area's	poetry	video	

High-Frequency Words

one	could	have	there
a	to	were	they
their	any	of	was
some	your	said	

In class one morning, Miss Green talked about poems. She explained that ideas for poems could sprout from all over. Different things can influence poets. There are poets that have seen a single meteor in the night sky and written about it. There are poets that have written poems about the cruel, cold January weather.

Miss Green asked each student in her class to create a poem that night. There were no rules.

Her students did not need to punctuate lines if they did not feel like it. These poems could be long or short. She told her class to make their poems about any idea that came to mind.

Leona is in Miss Green's class. As she rode her bus home, she tried thinking of a subject for her poem. As she looked out the bus window, Leona spotted a billboard. It was an ad for the town's museum. This museum has an annual music fest each year. On that billboard was a picture of a giant lion. That's it! She'd write a poem that stars a lion.

When Leona was home, she went right to her desk and started writing her lion poem. Her poem was titled "Champion of the Jungle." Leona handed in her poem to Miss Green the next day.

One morning three weeks later, Miss Green told her class that she had some news. "I submitted your poems to this area's annual poetry contest," Miss Green said. "And it turns out that Leona's poem is this year's winner!"

The class clapped for Leona! As the winner, her family got a free trip to the museum and a brand new video cam! Leona was glad she spotted that giant lion.

All Week Long

Written by Hilda Zadylak

Homophones

board/bored	here/hear	their/there
two/to/too	knew/new	flour/flower
road/rode	role/roll	aunt/ant
stair/stare	hour/our	week/weak
write/right		

High-Frequency Words

said	to	what	do
was	the	of	you
their	two	a	there
were	many	one	would
they	watched	full	sure

"I'm bored," Val said to Mom. "What can I do?"

It was the middle of summer. Val tapped her fingers on the board her mom was painting.

"Look at the world around you," said Mom. "Stop and take time to observe, and you will not be bored."

"How can I begin?" asked Val.

"What do you hear?" asked Mom. "Listen hard!"

Val did not hear too much at first. At last noises came to her ears. She heard the weak sound of cars whizzing along far away. Their motors hummed. Close by, birds sang songs and two bees buzzed. Mom's paintbrush made a whishing noise. Now here came a purring kitten. There were so many sounds to hear.

The next day, Val asked, "Now how can I observe?"

Mom knew what to ask. "What can you smell?"

Val sniffed the air. "Nothing," she said. But she found many new things to smell. One flower smelled like spice. Later Mom and Val mixed flour into cake batter. The freshly baked cake would smell sweet.

The next day as they rode in the car, Val grinned and asked, "What now?"

"What can you feel?" asked Mom.

The car seat felt hot. The glass window felt slick. Stones in the road felt sharp. Her puppy's nose was wet and cold. His fur felt soft and warm. Val liked how he felt.

Next Val tried out her taste buds. She played the role of a chef taste-testing foods. She crunched peanuts and chips. She tried pickles.

The banana she ate was sweet like cream, but a tart berry exploded in her mouth. She put jam on a hot fresh roll. That tasted best of all.

Friday was a day for seeing. Val and Aunt Lin strolled to the park. There were many things to stare at. Standing on a stair, Val watched a line of ants. Each ant held bits of leaves. Next Val and Aunt Lin sat down and watched a ballgame for an hour. It ended when a player struck out.

"Our day was fun!" Val told Mom when she returned home.

It had been a fun-filled week without even an echo of "I'm bored."

In her diary, Val would write, "The world is full of sounds, smells, tastes, feelings, and sights."

On Saturday, Val went outside first thing. She was sure the world had many more things to teach her, and she was right!

Brett's Day at the Inn

Homophones

new/knew	to/too
bored/board	inn/in
creaks/creeks	allowed/aloud
plains/planes	road/rode/rowed
main/mane	would/wood
hole/whole	knight/night

High-Frequency Words

to	a	sure	wasn't
was	the	there	been
one	of	come	they
where	would		

Brett woke up to a new day! And he knew one thing for sure. He wasn't going to be bored. Brett was spending the summer working hard at Gramps's inn. There was never a boring day at Gramps's! This cozy inn has been in Brett's family for years. One day, Brett might even own it too.

As Brett went down the steps to breakfast, an old board creaked. "That same old board creaks every day," Brett told himself. "I like that!"

After breakfast, Brett stood on the inn's porch and looked around. Gramps's inn sat next to a big lake in the middle of open plains. Creeks ran off the lake.

Brett squinted at the little landing strip down by the main road. This strip allowed small planes to come and go. That is how most visitors got to Gramps's. No planes had landed yet this morning.

Brett ran down to the inn's horse stable. Brett's favorite horse was Brownie, an old slow horse. Matt helped Brett saddle up Brownie. Brett rode her to Twisted Creek. Brett patted Brownie's mane. He tied her to a tree.

Gramps was waiting for Brett in a boat. They rowed to where they would work.

Yesterday, Gramps and Brett had dug up an old wood pole. Now they had to fill that hole with dirt. Brett and Gramps spent almost the whole morning filling it. As they worked, Gramps told a funny story about a knight in rusty armor. He chuckled aloud as he told it.

It was past noon when they finished. Brett and Gramps rowed back. Brett untied Brownie and he and Gramps walked the big old horse back to her stable. They saw a plane land on the strip. Gramps told Brett about plans for the rest of the day and night. There would be more work and then a cookout. It would not be a boring day!

Jobs

Homophones

be/bee	deer/dear	feet/feat
heel/heal	two/too/to	brakes/breaks
flea/flee	write/right	flour/flower
mail/male	sell/cell	soar/sore
high/hi		

High-Frequency Words

they	a	who	two
said	want	to	you
could	the	would	of
are	people	do	your

Marge and her pals discussed things they might be when they grow up.

"I might be a forest ranger," Marge told her pals. "I will protect dear, sweet animals like bunnies and deer."

"I might be a doctor who fixes feet," announced Candy. "If a person has a bad heel, I might heal it!"

"Feet! Those are two things that smell!" said Rachel. "I will fix car brakes, motors, and tires."

"Cars smell too," smiled Kim. "I might be a bee keeper!"

"I don't like bugs," shouted Joan. "Even the littlest flea makes me want to flee!"

"Well, I can tell you this," began Linda, "I want to be a writing teacher. I could help kids write the right way. That would be a neat feat."

"I will be a baker," explained Amy. "I will bake cookie after cookie out of flour and sweetener, each in the shape of a flower."

"Yum! I will be a mail person," explained Jess. "Many mailmen are male. I'll be a female mailman."

"As long as we're being silly," chimed in Sophie, "I might sell cell phones. Call me and I will tell you how to get a real deal!"

"I will call when I take breaks from flying," stated Grace. "I know that I will pilot planes when I get big. I will soar high in that sky!"

"Perfect!" shouted Gail. "I might be a flight attendant. I would say 'hi' as people got on that plane. But I would get comfy sneakers so my feet would not get sore."

"Nice! If your feet do get sore, you can see me!" yelled Candy. "I'll be your foot doctor and heal your heel!"

"Nice, but smelly!" cried Rachel.

All That Moms Do

Written by Elena Placido

/ö/ Vowel Patterns spelled *a, au, aw, al, augh, ough*

lawn	tall	walnut
thought	because	ought
always	caught	saw
calling	brought	squawking
sought	all	small
bought	walked	hall
taught		

High-Frequency Words

the	of	was	a
there	to	one	want
your	said	you	here
of	something	mother	again
what's	what		

At the end of the lawn in Jim's backyard was an old tall walnut tree. Jim's dad had made a house in it, and Jim often went there to think about things. As he sat and thought about stuff, he liked to hear the wind in the leaves, and see birds flutter from branch to branch.

One day Jim went to his treehouse because he did not want to clean his room.

"Your room is a mess," Mom had said. "I want you to clean it by lunchtime.

"No! No! No!" Jim thought. "It's my room and I ought to be free to keep it that way!"

He ran to his treehouse.

"I'll stay here for ten years," Jim said.

Jim sat in the tree and gazed at his house.

"Mom is always asking me to clean my room or make my bed," he grumbled to himself.

Just then, Jim caught sight of something outside the window.

"Chirp, chirp, chirp."

Jim saw a baby bird in a nest, calling for food.

A moment later a big bird landed beside the baby.

"This must be its mom," thought Jim.

The mother bird filled her baby's mouth with the food she brought back.

The little bird gobbled up its dinner. Then it started squawking again.

Mother bird soared off to find more food.

The big bird brought back more food and left again. The big bird sought more and more food. She always brought it back to her baby. Jim counted thirteen trips in all.

"That mom works hard," Jim thought.

And suddenly, he thought about his mom.

"My mom works hard also. She feeds me just like that mother bird feeds her small baby.

90

Jim got down from the tree and returned to his house. Without a sound he went up to his room and picked up his toys. Then he cleaned up the mess on his bed and desk.

Jim went to find his mom. She was making lunch from food she had bought.

"I'm starving," Jim told her.

"What's your room like?" asked his mom.

"Go see it," said Jim.

Jim's mom walked down the hall and came back a moment later smiling.

"Wow, Jim! What made you clean it?" she asked.

"A little bird taught me how!" Jim exclaimed.

Paul Shops for Mom

Vowel Patterns *a, au, aw, al, augh, ough*

August	Paul	bought	talked	baseball
walked	mall	thoughts	lawn	straw
thought	draw	chalks	drawings	also
taught	law	small	sought	saw
halted	dawn	brought	daughter	because
all				

High-Frequency Words

a	to	said	sure
anything	do	you	have
other	of	the	from

Mom has an August birthday. Paul bought a gift for her. Paul talked to his big sister Stella about it. "I bought Mom baseball cards," he said.

"I am not sure that's good!" replied Stella.

"Well, I walked around the mall and didn't find anything better to get," explained Paul. "Do you have other thoughts?

"Mom likes her lawn and garden," Stella told Paul. "Instead of baseball cards, perhaps she might like a straw hat to block the sun."

"That's a good thought!" nodded Paul.

"She also likes to sketch and draw," Stella pointed out. "Maybe you should have gotten her chalks for her drawings instead of cards."

"Those are also good thoughts," agreed Paul.

Then Stella reminded Paul that Mom taught law classes at a small university. "You might have sought a good teaching gift for her," Stella said.

Paul saw that might be true too. He started to say that, but halted. Instead he said, "But Mom likes baseball."

"Yes, Mom can talk about it from dawn to dark," agreed Stella.

"And she just brought her box of old baseball cards home from Granny's," said Paul.

"And Granny taught her daughter to like baseball," added Stella.

"That why aren't baseball cards a good gift?" asked Paul.

"Because I bought them too!" cried Stella.

Paul thought for a second. "Mom will like all the baseball cards she gets!" he announced.

Dawn and Baseball

Vowel Patterns _a, au, aw, al, augh, ough_

Walker	daughter's	baseball	Dawn	taught
small	tall	all	yawn	ought
because	ball	fought	thought	saw
caught	talk	fault	called	

High-Frequency Words

was	to	the	of	other
comes	they	do	their	into
one	could	would	a	lose
your	said	have	you	

Mrs. Walker coached her daughter's baseball team. Her daughter was Dawn. Mrs. Walker taught Dawn to play baseball when she was small. Now Dawn was tall and thin. She did not look like the star of her team, but she was. Her teammates bragged about her all the time.

"Other teams yawn when thin Dawn comes up to bat," explained Dawn's teammate Jill. "They think she will not do well. But those players ought to get set to run, because Dawn will smash that ball way over their heads!"

As coach of Dawn's team, Mrs. Walker tried to act like her coach and not like her mom. She treated Dawn like she treated all the kids. She taught them skills that helped them play better.

This season, Mrs. Walker's team fought into first place. They had one game left. If they could win it, Mrs. Walker's team would be champs!

This last game was a close one! Dawn came up to bat. If she made an out, this game would end and her team would lose. If she hit a home run, her team would win.

"Stay strong, Dawn," Mrs. Walker thought to herself.

Dawn swung hard at a pitch. The crowd saw the ball fly up, up, up! They saw it soar to the tall fence! Then they saw a fielder jump high! She caught the ball! Dawn was out. The game was over.

All her teammates came over to talk to Dawn. "It's not your fault, Dawn," Jill said.

Mrs. Walker, the coach, was proud of her team and Dawn! "We don't have to be the champs to stand tall," Mrs. Walker called.

But Mrs. Walker, the mom, was so sad for her daughter. She hugged Dawn and whispered, "You are still the best."

Heidi and Her Mom

Written by Matt Kooper

Word Lists
Vowel Patterns Spelled *ei, eigh*

Heidi	eight	either
neither	neigh	ceiling
Keith	neighbor	receive
weight	Neil	freight

High-Frequency Words

was	clothes	to	you
said	a	would	the
one	your	from	of
there	pretty	laugh	what

Heidi was just eight years old. At times, she didn't agree with Mom. And Mom didn't agree with her either. But Mom was right. Heidi didn't clean her room and left dirty clothes all over. Mom asked her to be neat and helpful. Heidi was neither.

At dinnertime, Heidi might act as if she didn't like Mom's cooking. She refused to eat everything.

"Maybe I'll just feed you hay," Mom said.

Heidi would just neigh like a horse. Mom would look at the ceiling and count to ten. Heidi would then eat, but not happily.

One day, Heidi's mom was not feeling well. She had to go see Doctor Keith, so she called a neighbor to sit with Heidi. But Heidi did not take this news well.

"I'm eight years old," said Heidi. "I don't need a babysitter!"

But Heidi secretly felt she did.

Mom told Doctor Keith how she was feeling. He checked her out.

"Your fever is high!" said Doctor Keith. "You must stay in bed for a week or so. You must take it easy. You will need to receive help from neighbors and family."

Mom hoped Heidi would help.

When Mom told Heidi that she was sick and needed to rest, Heidi felt bad for being so fussy lately.

"I'll help as much as I can, Mom," Heidi said. Then Heidi left for a bit and came back with a tray that had Mom's lunch. "I'll carry my weight at home from now on."

Mom felt proud of Heidi.

Mom had to spend much time in bed. Heidi sat with her. Heidi read to Mom. She even made up silly stories to tell Mom.

"There was a boy named Neil," began Heidi. "Neil lived on a freight train."

"A freight train?" giggled Mom. "That's pretty silly!"

They would laugh all day telling stories.

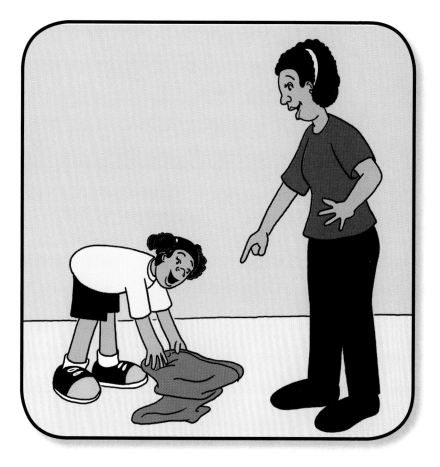

In a week, Mom felt much better. And Heidi had learned that it's much better to be helpful, rather than fussy all the time. She ate all her meals and cleaned up her dirty clothes.

And even when she did not agree with Mom, she still did what Mom asked. Sick or not, Mom needed her. And Heidi needed Mom!

Sleigh Rides

Vowel Patterns *ei, eigh*

sleigh	eight	ceiling
reins	weigh	weighs
weight	eighteen	eighty-eight
receive	neigh	

High-Frequency Words

the	a	to	they
there	of	do	though
two	one	from	said

In the wintertime, Dale and his family always take a trip to the same place. They go to a big resort in the middle of the state of Wisconsin. At this resort there are all sorts of things to do. The family can go ice-skating. They can go sledding. They can make snowmen. They can take sleigh rides. They can stay inside and play games. They can even swim at an indoor pool.

The thing that Dale likes most, though, is taking sleigh rides. He and his family get all bundled up under blankets as eight big horses pull an old red sleigh for miles and miles. Families get two choices on that sleigh ride. Families can either request that a sleigh ride go around the lake or that the sleigh take the forest trail. Dale likes the forest way better. It is so thick with fir trees that he can't see the sky. It's like there is a ceiling in that forest.

The sleigh driver yanks the reins and all his horses turn back for the resort. After his sleigh is back in its barn, that sleigh driver lets Dale pet all eight horses.

"How much do the horses weigh?" asks Dale.

"Each horse weighs nearly one thousand pounds," the driver tells Dale. "But this brown horse is much bigger. Its weight is close to eighteen hundred pounds!"

That's a lot! With all eight horses, that's around eighty-eight hundred pounds!

Dale got to feed the horses hay. That big brown horse seemed particularly glad to receive hay from Dale. That horse said, "Neigh!"

Dale and his family can't wait for these winter trips each year!

Miranda Turns Eight

Vowel Patterns *ei, eigh*

ceiling	eighth	eight
either	neither	neighbor
weigh	freight	weight
receive		

High-Frequency Words

was	having	of	to
the	said	do	you
your	have	one	other
could	here	sure	any

When Miranda woke up, she saw balloons all over her ceiling. At first she thought she was having a dream, but then she remembered. It was her eighth birthday! Miranda jumped out of bed and ran down to the kitchen. She spotted Mom.

"Morning, Mom," said Miranda. She decided to play it cool. "Do you know why my ceiling is filled with balloons?"

Mom just smiled. "Don't try that trick on me," replied Mom. "You know why those are on your ceiling. It's because you just turned eight!"

"That's right!" beamed Miranda. "Yay! I'm eight!"

"Since it's your birthday," explained Mom, "you have your breakfast choice. I can make either eggs with toast, or pancakes."

"Can't I have both?" asked Miranda.

"Nope. It's either one or the other," said Mom. Then she added, "Or if you prefer, I could make neither of them. You can have cereal."

Miranda selected eggs and toast. Then she asked Mom about her birthday party.

"What kinds of treats will we have when the neighbor kids get here?" asked Miranda.

"We'll have hot dogs on buns, loads of cole slaw, plus cake and ice cream," said Mom.

"Wow!" said Miranda. "I'm going to weigh a thousand pounds when this party is over. That is too much for my height! It'll take a freight train to haul all my weight around!"

"Just be sure to say thanks for any gifts you receive," reminded Mom.

All in all, Miranda's birthday party was a big success!

Selfish Shelly

Written by Stephen Grantland

Suffixes -y, -ish, -hood, -ment

shiny	frisky	stylish	childhood
sunny	enjoyment	neighborhood	wispy
yellowish	crunchy	yummy	cheesy
sticky	salty	thirsty	icy
refreshment	tricky	rocky	grumpy
childish	treatment	selfish	

High-Frequency Words

was	a	what
wanted	very	the
of	everyone	to
they	could	any
said	warm	sure
friends	one	been
having	there	

Shelly was a good girl, but she was a little spoiled. She almost always got what she wanted. When she asked for shiny new toys, she got them. When she asked for a frisky little puppy, she got it. When she asked for stylish dresses, she got them. She thought she had a very happy childhood.

On a sunny day in June, Matt had a party for the enjoyment of all the kids in his neighborhood. When the big day came, Shelly wore her sundress made of wispy, yellowish fabric. She came late, so everyone had to wait for her before they could start playing games.

Matt had a big tray of snacks. He had crunchy nuts, yummy popcorn, veggie sticks and cheesy dip, and sticky apple treats.

"I don't like any of that stuff," Shelly said with a sniff. "I'd rather eat something more healthful." Matt was sad that he had not made Shelly happy.

Salty snacks and warm sun made the kids thirsty. They went looking for icy cold refreshment. But Shelly had taken all the water, down to the very last drop. "Well, I filled my bottle. I'm sure I will be thirsty later," she said.

Later during the party, Shelly's friends crowded around the picnic table to solve a tricky puzzle. Shelly tried to squeeze in, but no one made room for her. Di even gave her an angry glance.

Shelly sat down on the rocky ground. First she felt grumpy, but then she began to think. "I acted childish and rude," Shelly admitted to herself. "My friends did not like the bad treatment I gave them. I wish I had been kinder. If I had, right now I'd be having fun with them!"

Matt saw that she looked sad. He came to her side. "I have been selfish," Shelly told him. "I will try to think of others from now on."

Matt stuck out his hand and helped her up. "You're still our friend," he said. "We can make room at the table for you."

There was room, and Shelly did have fun. After that, she tried hard not to be so selfish.

A Stormy Day

Suffixes -y, -ish, -hood, -ment

announcement	instrument	grayish
shiny	flashy	neighborhood
sunny	breezy	excitement
enjoyment	darkish	cloudy
rainy	chilly	grouchy
foolish	likelihood	gloomy
falsehood	greenish	stormy
windy	amazement	statements
grumpy	nasty	development
retirement		

High-Frequency Words

to	a	was	the
said	of	you	sure
there	today	do	any
your			

Professor Smiley made an announcement to reporters about a new weather forecasting instrument. He stood next to it. It was a grayish metal box that had shiny dials and flashy digital displays all over.

"This new instrument will forecast weather perfectly," explained the professor to reporters.

117

Professor Smiley then hit a switch. The box started to hum and dials started to spin and point. The professor read digital displays.

"In this neighborhood, it will be sunny and breezy all day," Professor Smiley said with excitement. "It will be a nice day for all kinds of outdoor enjoyment. Go fly a kite or play ball."

Reporter Heather Rose looked at the sky behind the professor. It looked darkish and cloudy. "Are you sure our weather will not be rainy and chilly?" she asked.

Professor Smiley took his glasses off and looked a bit grouchy. "It's almost foolish to ask that!" he exclaimed. "This instrument tells me there is no likelihood for gloomy weather today. This instrument is not capable of falsehood."

As the professor spoke, the sky behind him turned greenish and stormy. A windy gust whipped his hat off. Big drops of rain started to fall. The professor looked up in amazement. Then he and the reporters ran for shelter.

"Do you have any more statements about your weather forecasting instrument?" yelled Reporter Rose as she ran next to Professor Smiley.

"Yes," said the grumpy professor. "Thanks to this nasty development, this weather forecasting instrument is now in retirement!"

Messy Jim

Suffixes -y, -ish, -hood, -ment

chilly	windy	rainy	neighborhood
sloppy	muddy	ready	thirsty
icy	enjoyment	messy	dirty
shiny	selfish	foolish	soapy
slimy	snappy	improvement	sticky
statement	darkish	amazement	childhood
funny			

High-Frequency Words

come	the	a	was	some
from	of	said	to	were
there	they	why	off	one
your				

"Jim, come home," yelled Mom out the window. "It's getting chilly."

After a windy, rainy day, the weather was better. So Jim and some neighborhood kids played football on a sloppy, muddy field. When Mom called, Jim ran home.

"I'm home, Mom!" Jim yelled as he stepped inside.

"Dinner will be ready soon," called Mom from the basement. "Better get cleaned up."

Jim was so thirsty! Without removing his dirty sneakers, he grabbed an icy drink from the fridge. Jim's enjoyment of his drink ended when he turned around and saw messy, dirty footprints on Mom's shiny tile. "Yikes! I did that!" said Jim to himself. He felt selfish and foolish.

Jim grabbed a mop and a bucket of soapy water. He had to clean those slimy prints before Mom saw them. He had better make it snappy!

Jim wiped the tiles by the fridge. Soon they were clean. That was an improvement! Then Jim turned around. There were fresh sticky, dirty footsteps on the tile! How did they get there?

Gloomy Jim wiped away those prints too. As he wiped, he backed up to the fridge. When the tile before him was clean, he exclaimed. "I am finished at last!"

But that statement was not true. As Jim turned around, he saw more darkish, muddy prints by the fridge! How? Why?

Then Jim looked down. To his amazement, he had forgotten to take off his sneakers! He kept making new messy prints.

Then he saw Mom looking at him. "This will be one of my favorite stories of your childhood!" she said with a big grin.

Jim looked at his feet. This was funny!

At the Zoo

Written by Callie Terote

/ü/Spelled *oo, ew, ue, ui*

zoo	school	soon	Cooper
Rooney	cool	Sue	raccoon
food	fruit	noodles	bamboo
true	chew	shoots	

/ů/Spelled *oo, u*

Cook	Brooke
shook	bush
put	

High-Frequency Words

was	to	a
some	wanted	could
said	do	you
the	friend	eye
of	live	they
one	their	

121

Josh dressed quickly. His long wait was almost over! Today was his class trip to City Zoo.

At nine sharp, a big school bus parked at Cook School. Josh and Brooke got on first. Soon everybody else joined them. Some children began playing wildly. Cooper jumped up on his seat. Ashley shouted loudly. Josh wasn't unruly. He just wanted to focus on zoo sights he'd see.

"Quiet, please!" Miss Rooney called.

At last Josh and Brooke could hear themselves think.

"I'm excited about seeing tigers," Brooke said happily. "They're the animals I like best. Which do you like best, Josh?"

"You will find out soon," Josh replied. He smiled shyly at Brooke. Josh didn't really like keeping secrets. But talking too much about the animal might bring bad luck. He hoped he'd find it playing outside. Last time, the animal had hidden in its cool, dark cave. Josh could hardly see his furry friend.

At City Zoo, a helpful zookeeper named Sue greeted Miss Rooney's class. She began showing the excited children zoo animals. They saw lions, tigers, camels, and monkeys. Josh liked them all. At each stop, Brooke asked, "Isn't that the animal you like best, Josh?" Each time, Josh replied, "No."

At long last Sue led everybody to the animal
Josh liked best. Just as Josh had hoped, it sat
outdoors. It was black and white and quite big.
A big black mark circled each eye.

"It looks like a large raccoon!" Martin shouted.

"It looks like a gentle grizzly bear!" Ginny
yelled.

126

"It's not a raccoon or a bear, but it has traits of both. It's a giant panda! Which food do you think Pete Panda likes most?" Sue asked.

"Fruit?" Kevin asked. Sue shook her head.

"Meat? Noodles?" Jane asked. Sue shook her head twice.

"Leaves from a lilac bush?" Kate asked.

Josh just had to speak up. "Bamboo," he said.

"That's true," Sue nodded. "Lots of bamboo trees grow in China where pandas live. Pandas chew bamboo shoots, or tiny branches. They chew bamboo leaves as well. Aren't pandas picky? Bamboo is one of the few foods they'll put in their mouths."

Soon everybody got back on the bus. "Now we all know which animal you like best, Josh," said Brooke. She gave Josh a high five. "Cool!"

Kat's Kite

Vowel Sounds in *moon* and *foot*

new	flew	soon	blew	spool
wooden	took	pulled	good	stood
looked	zoomed	bluest	blue	school's
roof	fruit	pool	cool	zoo
moon	knew	true	grew	cruise
spacesuit	push	crew	shook	clue
too				

High-Frequency Words

a	into	the	of
was	could	another	would
what	to	one	from
other	their	you	

As Kat ran fast, her new kite flew up behind her. Soon it blew a few more yards up into the wind. Kat had a spool of string on the wooden stick in her hands. As she let that stick turn, her kite really took off. It unwound the spool of string higher and higher. It pulled at the stick as it did. Kat thought that was a good feeling.

Kat stood and looked as her kite zoomed up and down a bit in the bluest, blue sky. Then she sat on the ground and held the stick. Her kite looked as if it flew right over her school's roof now. That seemed far!

Kat wished she could tie on another spool of string. Then her kite could go higher and farther out. Might another spool help it fly over the fruit trees and swimming pool south of her school? That would be cool! Might a third spool of string make her kite reach high over the zoo? Might more spools help her kite reach the moon?

Kat knew that could not happen. But she knew what was true. She enjoyed the thrill of flying her kite!

As her kite danced high over her, Kat thought about flying. When she grew up, would she fly? Would she cruise the skies as a jet pilot? Would she put on a spacesuit and push a crew to the moon and stars? And would Kat one day look down from high? Would she see what her kite sees? Would she see other kids flying their kites in the sky below her?

The spool of string shook a bit. The kite quickly flew up and down in the sky. Was that a clue? Was her kite saying, "Yes, Kat, you will fly high too!"

Balloons!

Vowel Sounds in *moon* and *foot*

balloon	pulls	blue	soon	good-bye
few	too	true	good	flew
wooden	zoom	smooth	troops	notebooks
look	crews	tools	news	coolness
fooled	useful	put	clues	suit

High-Frequency Words

to	you	a	of	your
into	the	there's	do	they
some	were	ones	people	from
have	other	give	one	

Has this ever happened to you? A balloon pulls out of your hand and drifts into the blue sky. Soon there's not a thing you can do but wave good-bye to that balloon! Don't feel too bad. That's happened to quite a few people.

Most balloons are flimsy things. It's true that they look good and are fun for a bit. Then balloons pop, go flat, or at times, escape!

But not all balloons are toys. Some are created to work hard for people. The first working balloons were ones that people flew in—and still do. These balloons are filled with gas that helps them float high in the sky. Passengers stand in wooden baskets that hang from these balloons. At times, strong winds blow these balloons and they zoom too fast. Smooth rides are best.

Before planes, humans used these balloons to travel and explore. Armies even used them long ago. Spies flew over enemy troops and filled notebooks with what they saw.

Shiny weather balloons fly into space. These balloons do not have crews. They have electronic tools that send news about our planet's heat, coolness, rains, and winds. At times, these balloons show up in TV news reports. People can be fooled. They think these shiny things are spaceships from other planets!

Some useful balloons never really travel. They are put on poles or towers to give plane pilots clues about how winds are blowing.

One working balloon you may wish to use is a normal balloon filled with water. Use it on hot days when you have on a swimming suit. Have fun!

A Circus Life for Ben

Written by Jenna Borman

Schwa

ago	family	Benjamin	around	travel
seven	mountain	afraid	circus	about
famous	marble	juggled	moment	breakfast

High-Frequency Words

a	of	there
was	you	wanted
to	the	would
water	one	coming
some	have	been
said	into	they
everywhere	what	were

Long ago a family of bears lived in Berry
Woods. There was Mama Bear, Papa Bear, and
little Harry Benjamin Bear. It was a big name for
a tiny bear. But Ben, as everybody called him,
had big dreams.

Life was quiet in Berry Woods. It was way too
quiet, if you asked Ben!

Ben wanted to travel around the world. He
dreamed about sailing the seven seas. He would
zip over bright blue water and see huge whales
spout. He dreamed of climbing Earth's tallest
mountain. He would plant his family's flag on it.
He dreamed of exploring the darkest jungle. All
wild animals would be afraid of him.

Then one day, Ben saw a poster. "A circus!" cried Ben. The Flying Bear Circus was coming to Berry Woods!

Ben liked everything about circuses. Now he dreamed about being a high-wire performer or a trapeze artist. He also dreamed about being a famous clown. A circus life was the life for Ben.

Ben thought, "I must join the circus!"

Ben packed his lucky marble and some honey. He tiptoed out of his house so Mama and Papa Bear would not wake up. He walked until he was tired. After a little rest, he reached the circus.

"We have been waiting for you," said the Circus Master.

Ben was a hit at the circus. He balanced on his head and juggled balls with his feet.

He swung gracefully on a trapeze. He let go, and the crowd gasped. At just the right moment, he grabbed his swing. Ben was safe!

He climbed into a tiny truck with a clown, and they drove around, honking the horn. Everybody cheered wildly. "Hurray for Ben!"

Ben traveled everywhere with the circus. Its train chugged over mountains and into valleys. The circus went around the world. Ben was a hot item! Tickets sold out in Paris and Rome and Calcutta.

But Ben missed Mama and Papa Bear. He felt sad. "I must go home," he cried. And that is what he did.

Mama and Papa were happy to see Ben. While they fixed breakfast, he told them all about life in the circus. Mama and Papa smiled happily and didn't seem surprised at all.

"Now will you stay home with us, Ben?" they asked.

"Yes," said Ben. "Home is the place for me!"

Sylvester's Notes

Schwa

circus	caboose	remember	asparagus
elephants	traveling	aquarium	marble
weather	hamster	hammers	forgot
afraid	forget	even	apples
children's	baker	pretzels	idea
little	paper	pencil	after
along	decorated	bubble	tickets
kitchen	helpers	oven	order
center	before		

High-Frequency Words

the	to	a
was	would	could
of	said	have
into		

Sylvester sat at his desk in the circus train's caboose. Sylvester felt stressed. He had so much to remember. Running a circus was hard!

Right now Sylvester had to get asparagus for his elephants, clean his shark's traveling aquarium, shine the marble steps used for dog tricks, check the weather, feed his hamster, get hammers for his crew, and more.

Sylvester's problem was that he forgot a lot! He was afraid he might forget even more! He needed a way to remember to get apples for his horses, get ready for the children's show, and ask Baker Bob to whip up fresh pretzels.

How would Sylvester remember all this? Then an idea hit him. He could write things on little notes. He would stick those notes on his desk.

Sylvester found sticky yellow pieces of paper. With his pencil, he wrote note after note on those papers. He stuck them along his desk's edges. In no time, his desk was decorated with yellow notes that said things like *get more bubble wrap, print tickets for next show, have kitchen helpers clean oven,* and *order more yellow paper notes.*

Sylvester had just stuck that last note on his desk when his circus train started. In seconds, it raced along the tracks. Wind blew into the caboose's side window. Wind blew Sylvester's yellow notes out the caboose's back window.

Sylvester got up and closed the windows. Then he sat down and wrote a new note and tacked it in the center of his desk. It said *Close the windows before the train starts.*

Picnic Poster

Schwa

biggest	event	summer	annual
Village	different	adult	directed
assistant	children's	Mayor	poster
purple	over	eleven	circus
weather	balloon	circus	tickets
ahead	forgot	forget	every

High-Frequency Words

the	of	was	a
one	to	would	there
could	said	you	who
why			

The biggest event of the summer was the annual Grove Village picnic. Each year a different adult directed it. A village child was always named as that adult's assistant. The child helped get children's games ready.

This summer, Mayor Burris planned the picnic. The child helping her was Andy Johnson.

One of Andy's jobs was to design the picnic poster. The poster told about the children's games. Andy took a design for the poster to Smithson's Print Shop. Mr. Smithson printed these posters every year. And he always worked with the child assistant.

This year's poster was bright white with deep purple printing. Mr. Smithson looked over Andy's design. Andy's poster explained that the picnic was at Center Park. It would start at eleven and end at dusk. There would be circus rides. Tents would be set up in case of bad weather.

Andy's poster also listed times for each of the kids' games including races, kids' bingo, and balloon tosses. The poster announced that lunch tickets could be bought ahead of time.

Andy thought he did a good job. His poster even had a drawing of kids running. "Nice poster, Andy. But read this note," Mr. Smithson said.

He handed Andy an old wrinkled paper. It said *You forgot to put the date on the poster!*

"Yikes!" yelled Andy.

"Don't feel bad," explained Mr. Smithson. "Kids who make this poster forget the date every year! That's why I save this old wrinkled note!"

Chase Takes a Vacation

Written by J. A. Vezzetti

Syllables *-tion, -sion, -ion, -ture, -ive, -ize*

active	vacation	adventures
decision	inventive	picture
station	substitution	visualize
future		

High-Frequency Words

was	the	wasn't	a
would	have	of	to
only	could	gone	there
said	very	wanted	water

145

Henry Tucker was the unhappiest boy in Port Town. His cat Chase had disappeared six weeks ago. At first Henry wasn't worried. Chase was active and often took a vacation, but he always came back in a few days. Henry thought that Chase would have lots of good stories to tell about his adventures—if only Chase could talk!

After Chase had been gone for three days,
Henry made a decision to search. First he looked
carefully in all the places that Chase might hide.
Chase wasn't in the shed in the garden or in the
maple tree by the fence. He wasn't under the
porch of the red house on Vine Street.

Chase wasn't in the boxes behind the bookstore or by the food market. He wasn't in the tall grass or under the hedges around the pond.

Next Henry was inventive. He posted signs all over town. The signs had the word *Missing,* a picture of Chase, and a phone number. Henry waited by the phone, but no one called.

As the days went by, Henry grew discouraged. His dad took him to the police station and the animal pound. There were lots of cats there, but no Chase. Dad said, "Maybe you want to get another cat."

A substitution for Chase? Henry could not visualize that. Chase was much too special a cat.

Henry thought about Chase all the time. He recalled that Chase often sat on Henry's desk while he worked. Chase gracefully tucked his paws and watched Henry with big green eyes. Now the desk looked empty. At night in bed Chase would curl up right next to Henry. It was a bit uncomfortable at first, but Henry got used to it. Now his bed felt very lonely.

150

Cat ownership was often hard and messy, but all that Henry recalled now was Chase purring and rubbing on his legs. Henry had disliked it when Chase misbehaved. Now Henry wished that Chase would come back and misbehave as much as he wanted. Henry slumped lower on the steps. The future did not look bright.

Suddenly Chase reappeared in the yard. Unprepared for this sight, Henry didn't move. Then he grabbed and hugged the cat tightly. Chase squirmed free and licked his ruffled fur. He looked at Henry as if to say, "How about refreshments?"

Henry smiled and refilled the food and water dishes. Chase was home.

Talkative Millie

Final syllables –tion, -ion, -ture, -ive, ize

television	stations	population
picture	adventures	active
Talkative	inventive	mention
realize	decision	visualize
future		

High-Frequency Words

the	was	any	other
of	to	one	said
a	they	could	their
many	people	who	buy
do	some	you	again
anything			

Millie Owens had the most popular daytime television show in America. It was on more TV stations than any other show. All of America's population knew her. Her picture was on billboards and in magazines. Her fans read all about her adventures, both on television and in her active, exciting real life.

153

On Mondays, Millie Owens's show was always about cooking. Talkative Millie joked and told stories as she showed her fans how to prepare her new favorite dish.

One Monday, Millie baked an inventive new kind of casserole. When she lifted the hot dish out of the oven, Millie happened to mention that her oven mitts looked worn out. Talkative Millie did not even realize she had said it.

But across America, hundreds of thousands of Millie's fans realized she did. And most of those fans made a decision. They decided to send Millie new oven mitts. Fans could visualize Millie using their oven mitts on TV.

A few fans made oven mitts and sent them to Millie. Many, many fans bought mitts and sent them. Soon TV stations across America had boxes and boxes of mitts for Millie. For weeks, truckloads of mitts arrived at Millie's studio. People who really needed new oven mitts could not buy them. Stores had run out!

Millie did not know what to do with those mitts. She sent some to needy people, but the rest she saved. You can see them in Millie Owens's Museum of Oven Mitts!

And in the future, talkative Millie will never again mention on TV anything she might need!

Lester's Pictures

Final syllables –tion, -ion, -ture, -ive, ize

visualize	pictures	decision
station	motion	action
conclusion	realize	adventures
active	vacations	population
nature	creatures	expensive
champion	television	inventive
imagination		

High-Frequency Words

was	said	to	many
a	would	of	want
do	the	been	what

Jill told Lester she was ready to paint. Lester said he was ready too. But first he had to explain to Jill his problem. "I visualize too many different pictures to paint! It's difficult to make a decision!"

Lester then said he might paint a train zooming past a railroad station. But then trains made him think about how roller coasters in motion looked. Lester exclaimed, "Fast moving things thrill me. I like action paintings!"

This conclusion made Lester realize he would paint the kinds of adventures he liked best. "I enjoy active vacations," Lester said. "I want to do things that most of the population will not do. I want to climb rocky cliffs and swim under deep seas."

Lester added that he enjoyed nature, but not in city parks. Instead, he liked jungles crawling with frightening creatures. That would make an exciting painting!

Lester was quiet for a second. Jill started to speak, but Lester suddenly said, "I also visualize creating pictures showing expensive racecars. A painting that shows me in a speeding racecar might be perfect. I might paint myself dressed like a racecar champion I saw on television."

Jill looked a little angry. Lester realized he hadn't asked Jill about her painting plans. His inventive imagination had been in the way! Lester quickly asked Jill what she wanted to paint.

"Lester!" she yelled, "I want to paint the backyard fence, just like Dad told us to do!"

Lester looked embarrassed. Then he said, "Let's paint it fast and make it an adventure!"

Invisible Uncle Mycroft

Written by Andy Basset

Prefixes *im-, in-*

impolite	independent	impassable
indecisive	immobile	invisible
imperfect	impossible	

High-Frequency Words

to	a	they
what	was	the
would	their	could
one	said	of
you	wanted	buy
where	again	your

157

Uncle Mycroft had invited Brad and his sister Ella to spend a week with him. Brad and Ella had never met Uncle Mycroft. They didn't mean to be impolite, but they had lots of questions. Why did he ask to see them now? What was he like?

"My brother Mycroft is an inventor," Dad explained. "I speak to him by phone all the time, but I haven't seen him for twenty years."

This would be their first independent trip without Mom and Dad. They could not get away from work, so Ella and Brad traveled alone by bus.

They got a big surprise when they saw Uncle Mycroft's house. His house was old, and its walk was nearly impassable.

Brad sighed, and Ella took a deep breath. She wasn't indecisive. She rang the bell.

The door creaked open, but no one was in sight. All Brad and Ella saw was a room full of dusty furniture. They stood immobile.

"I'm over here, children," said a deep voice.

Brad and Ella looked in the direction of the voice. They saw an empty armchair.

"Don't be alarmed," said the voice. "You can't see me because I'm invisible!"

160

So that was why no one had seen Uncle Mycroft for twenty years!

A long time ago he had invented a potion that made a person invisible. The potion worked, but it was slightly imperfect. Uncle Mycroft had not found a way to reverse it. He wanted Brad and Ella to buy the things he needed for more tests.

All that week Brad and Ella went shopping for Uncle Mycroft. And all that week he tested his new potion. It seemed impossible to get right.

At last it was ready. Uncle Mycroft took a large spoonful. Nothing happened.

Suddenly Brad and Ella heard a small voice. "It worked—well, sort of."

Brad and Ella gasped. Where was Uncle Mycroft this time?

"Look down, kids," called a cheerful voice.

They looked down and there was Uncle Mycroft. Yes, they could see him now. But he was just six inches tall.

"Not perfect, but a good start," said the tiny uncle.

At the end of the week, Brad and Ella told Uncle Mycroft that they'd visit him again whenever he needed them.

Mom and Dad met the kids at the bus station.

"Tell us all about your trip," Dad said. "What's Uncle Mycroft like now?"

"Well, right now he's kind of like you," Ella said, "but a little shorter."

164

Sadie's Size

Prefixes *im-, in-*

impossible	impolite	immature
invisible	inattentive	inside
invited	insisted	impractical
inform	independent	incapable

High-Frequency Words

was	four	some	bother
were	a	there	one
though	to	could	the
of	who	they	their
another	would	other	give
where	any		

Sadie was almost in grade four. But some kids thought that was impossible. Sadie was small. She looked like she might be in second grade.

Being small did not bother Sadie. Even when impolite kids teased her about it, she wasn't upset. She knew those kids were a bit immature.

There was one strange thing about being small, though. At times, kids and even adults did not seem to see Sadie. She felt invisible then. That could be a bad thing when she was playing baseball or basketball. Invisible Sadie was always the last kid chosen for a team.

It used to be that way for soccer, too, until kids saw how good Sadie was. And that is when being small and almost invisible was a nice thing. Some soccer players were inattentive to Sadie's movements on the field. When she realized that, Sadie could cut inside of those players, steal the ball, and kick a goal!

Kids who knew Sadie always invited her to play soccer. They insisted she be on their side!

There was another nice thing about being small and almost invisible. When neighborhood kids played hide and seek, Sadie would always win. She could hide in places that would be impractical for most kids. After Sadie hid for a while, other kids would give up trying to find her. That's when she would pop up and inform them where she was.

Sadie did not know how big she would be when she grew up. Big or small, Sadie would always be independent and happy. She was incapable of being any other way.

Ms. Impossible

Prefixes im-, in-

immobile	inside	impossible
incapable	indecisive	incredible
insist	impolite	improper
incomplete	insulted	invalid
inform	inattentive	

High-Frequency Words

was	though	a	there
who	to	the	of
you	do	said	want
could			

The sun was up, but Annie still slept soundly. In fact, she was totally immobile in bed. Yet even though her body was still, a lot was going on inside her head. In there, Annie was starring in a terrific dream.

In her dream, Ms. Impossible, who looked just like Annie, was rushing to help a man trapped inside a car. The car hung on the edge of a cliff.

The man was incapable of getting out. But Ms. Impossible flew down and saved him.

"How did you do that?" asked the man. "That was impossible!"

Ms. Impossible smiled. Seconds later, she spotted a shy, indecisive cat stuck in a tree. Ms. Impossible made an incredible leap and grabbed the cat. "Ms. Impossible, I insist on paying you for saving Fluffy!" said the cat's owner.

"I don't want to sound impolite," replied Ms. Impossible. "But it's improper to pay superheroes!"

Then a different voice asked Ms. Impossible for aid. "My schoolwork is incomplete. Can you help me finish it?"

Ms. Impossible was shocked and insulted. This was an invalid request! She had to inform this person that superheroes did not help inattentive kids finish school assignments!

Just then Ms. Impossible felt a hand shaking her and she could hear the same voice. "Annie, please get up and help me!"

Sleepy Annie slowly looked up at the voice. It was her little sister, Kate. "You are impossible to wake up!" said Kate.

Impossible? Annie rolled over and smiled.

Mike the Medic

Written by Renee McLean

Related words

medic/medical	act/action	sign/signal
hand/handle	cloth/clothes	safe/safety
breath/breathe	finally/finished	able/ability

High-Frequency Words

a	people	who
have	they	to
gives	the	many
where	one	anyone
their	clothes	sure
do	very	

This is Mike. He is a medic. A medic helps
people who have medical problems before they
can get to a doctor. Mike gives first aid when
people are hurt or sick. Medics help take injured
or sick people to the hospital so that they can get
medicine and other help needed.

Mike works for the fire department. Like many
medics, he is a firefighter too. Mike sleeps at the
firehouse. But Mike won't stay asleep for long.
The alarm tells Mike that it is time to wake up and
get to work. He gets dressed quickly and rushes
to his truck. It's time for action!

The truck has lights and sirens that signal drivers to pull over to the side of the road. Bright, flashing lights and loud, wailing sirens are signs that this truck needs to get someplace fast. Cars pull over and stop to make way for this fire truck.

When the truck gets to the place where help is needed, the firefighters see smoke. A house is on fire! Mike and the other firefighters act quickly. Mike grabs the handle of his first-aid kit with one hand and blankets with his other hand. While other firefighters put out the fire, Mike checks to see if anyone is hurt.

Mike sees a family standing on the sidewalk. They look cold and frightened. Their clothes smell smoky and their faces are sooty. But everybody is safe. They had put cloth over their noses and mouths, which protected them from smoke. Mike checks them out and wraps blankets around them to keep them warm.

The fire is out at last. Now Mike helps the firefighters. Tim feels sick from heat and smoke. He cannot catch his breath. Mike puts a mask on his face to help him breathe clean air while he rests. Tim will see a doctor to make sure he is healthy and safe. Marla needs Mike's help too. She fell inside the house and cut her arm. Mike works hard looking after these brave safety workers.

When they are finished, Mike and the other firefighters return to the station. Mike can finally get back to sleep. He is really tired now, but he is also happy that he is able to do such good work. His ability to help people every day makes Mike very proud.

Finally Finished

Related Words

music/musical	act/action
voice/vocal	fun/funny
medical/medicine	breath/breathe/breathing
able/ability	finally/finished

High-Frequency Words

from	wasn't	very	the
was	to	what's	doing
a	do	you	said
what	some	they	have
buying			

Kevin walked away from his music lesson, but he wasn't feeling very musical. Across the street, his pal Albert spotted him. Albert could tell that Kevin was unhappy. Albert had to act now to help his pal.

The first action Albert took was to cross the street. His next action was to ask, "What's wrong, Kevin?"

"Umm," replied Kevin. "I was doing my vocal exercises and my singing voice is acting funny."

"Is that a medical problem?" asked Albert. "Perhaps a doctor and medicine might help."

"Nope, it's not medical," explained Kevin.

"How about a breathing problem?" Albert asked. "Do you breathe correctly when you sing?"

"Yes, my breath control is good when I sing," said Kevin sadly. "My voice just sounds funny."

"But not in a fun way?" asked Albert, jokingly.

"Not to me!" exclaimed Kevin.

Albert thought for a bit. Then he said, "Help me understand this. You are still able to sing, right?"

"Well, that's the problem. My singing ability isn't what it could be," explained Kevin. "Some people sing well. They have nice voices. I finally realized that I don't."

"What will you do?" asked Albert.

"Well, I have finally finished taking singing lessons!" exclaimed Kevin with a smile. "But I am buying drums!"

Desert Hiking

Related Words

thermos/thermometer   hand/handy
safe/safety   vision/visors/visible
cloth/clothes   signaled/signs
sense/sensitive/sensation

High-Frequency Words

the	said	have
of	to	their
they	were	why
you	your	what

Jack and Randy hiked with Dad in the desert. Jack looked at the small thermometer in his hand. "Wow! This handy little digital device shows 98 degrees," he said. "I'm glad we played it safe and have an extra thermos of cool water."

"Safety is important when hiking in the desert," agreed Dad.

"Looking at this little thermometer makes me feel even hotter," announced Jack. "I'm going to hide it out of my sight for a while."

Dad and his boys continued on their walk. They were glad they wore visors and sunglasses to protect their vision in the bright sun.

Suddenly Dad signaled the boys to stop and be silent. He pointed to a tiny lizard. The boys looked as the lizard scampered away.

"Hey," said Randy. "That's why we keep seeing signs along this trail with a picture of a lizard. The trail we're on is called Lizard Trail."

"We saw visible proof!" said Jack.

The hikers continued. "Whew," said Jack. "Even in the thin cloth of this hiking shirt, I sense that the temperature has climbed up."

"I feel it too," replied Randy. "My clothes are soaked with sweat. I'm too sensitive to heat. Why don't you check your thermometer, Jack?"

Jack pulled out the thermometer and said, "Great. It shows 75 degrees! That's better."

"What!" exclaimed Dad. "My body has a real sensation of higher heat, not lower."

"Well, that's probably because I hid the thermometer in the thermos of cool water," smiled Jack. "But just seeing this thermometer say 75 degrees makes me feel much cooler!"